Half Full, Or Half

A Collection of

Second Edition

Ana Monnar

Readers Are Leaders U.S.A.

Miami, FL

Dedication

This book is dedicated in loving memory to my husband, Octavio Monnar. We were blessed with over 25 years of love, trust and respect to one another. Thanks to our matrimony, we were later blessed with three children, Alberto, Anna and Alexander who were a gift from God.

Acknowledgments

I wish to express my gratitude and thanks to the people and organizations that made a difference. Their kindness, help and generosity were blessings from above.

Sts. Peter and Paul Catholic School and Church

Sts. Peter and Paul's Faculty and Staff

Sts. Peter and Paul Home and School Association

The Elvira A. Menendez

Family Crisis Scholarship Fund

Maria Verdeja School of the Arts

Miami Hoops for Youths

Kiwanis of Little Havana

The Miami Heat

Wolverine Summer Camp at Belen Jesuit

Coral Gables Youth Center

My Loving Family and Friends

Without them, my children's lives would have changed even more during a time of family crisis. I thank God for everything, my faith, family, friends, health, home and for sending me the Angels mentioned above.

~iii~

Table of Contents

~x~

Introduction

This book is a literary piece intended to inspire, and educate most audiences. When reading or reciting a poem, try to use intonation, expression and bring the poem to life. Giggle, if it's funny, show happiness, pain and sorrow when it calls for those emotions. The love of reading and writing is acquired by a large number of people of all ages. Some attain it from a very young age, while others experience it later on in life. The topics expressed in the poems were such as faith, hope, character education, determination, responsibility, kindness, Alzheimer's disease, nature, famous inventors, unity, plus much more.

I. *From the Heart*

Half Full, Or Half Empty?

When you see a glass that is halfway,

Do you see it half full or half empty?

I will tell you what I see,

I see a glass that is half full.

Then, I thank God for quenching my thirst

And I continue to count my blessings.

For you see, I have faith, a family and a roof over my head.

That is more than many others might have,

For some are hungry, homeless and lost.

You might have loved ones that are very ill,

But count your blessings for the good times.

You might have loved ones that have died,

But be grateful for the memories.

Thank God for what you have and be grateful!

Count your blessings, be grateful, do right.

With God all things are possible.

Thank you God for everything

~15~

Mother

Mother, dear mother

I would not trade you for any other

Asker, loaner, teacher, mourner

I love you mother! I love you mother!

My loving mother loves her four children
Not one more than the other
Three girls and one boy

Father

Thank you for always believing in me
You gave me courage to conquer what I wished for
After hard work I earned my degree
I finally realized that I was born to be a teacher
Thank you father for your generosity
After the gift of love and support
I was blessed with curiosity
Also with a father that was a good sport

Brother

When I think of you my dear brother
I think of a perfect ten
For you are like no other
I thank God for you again and again

Sisters

My two sisters I love dearly
Nothing could come between us
Our love is quite sincere
There is not a thing we could not discuss

Dogs Are Not Pets, They Are Family Members

Four Yorkshire Terriers Tiny, Holly, Charlie, Joy
You gave us many years of happiness
Filled with love, affection and unconditional love
How we took care of you
At night the bed was never crowded
With the four bundles of joy
Snuggling close to their masters
Many years of togetherness
until each one of you grew quite old
at the end, each one of you crossed the rainbow bridge
straight to paradise where you saw the white dove
Someday when the time is right
we shall meet again
what joy, peace and tranquility
Never again any disasters
From then on just peace and blessings
just enjoying the calm
God's good will shall give us wings
to protect the ones we love.

~20~

A Tribute to Bill

Young and full of life
You left one morning thinking you would come back
A dreadful accident caused by a housewife
Now your body rests under a brass plaque
Your kindness and humor will always be remembered
May God keep you in Heaven where there is to ponder
The Angels are blessed to have you as a member
One day you will meet again
With your loved ones that were left on Earth
Only time will heal the pain
Let God bless us with spiritual rebirth
Please guide us and free us from distress
Let Heaven's Angels bring us peace
For peace and tranquility bring great success
Cease and put an end to the breach of peace

It Doesn't Matter

It doesn't matter if you are short or tall
When you are visiting a mall
It doesn't matter if you are thin or stout
When you get ready to shout
It doesn't matter what color your skin might be
As long as you can live free
It doesn't matter if you are rich or poor
When you leave your house and lock the door
We are all special to God
Whether or not we drive a hot rod
We are all special to the ones that love us
Whether we walk or take the bus
What does matter is what is inside
Beauty comes from within
Be humble and don't have too much pride
Be kind and hold up your chin

Ballerina Girl

You are so beautiful my ballerina girl
Dancing sweetly since age four
Tiptoe, twirl, swirl
Always dancing in and out the door
Your lovely teachers
Have taught you grace
Your lovely features
And your warm embrace
I love you daughter
You were a gift from God
When you swim in a body of water
From afar you just nod
You are full of talent
You love to play basketball, run and read
Lively and spirited with such gallant
Your love and affection I will always need

Believe In Yourself

Believe in yourself
Always try your best
Put maximum effort
In every task you take
Be enthusiastic
Courteous and kind
You know you can do it
If you give it a try

Determination

Be passionate about what you do
be consistent and have determination
be responsible and reliable too
Put maximum effort with or without perspiration

Say Something Nice

Some people get a kick out of putting people down
Their parents should have told them,
"Say something nice and don't make them frown."
Offer nice words to make citizens feel like a gem
Think of other people's feelings
Be kind and say something nice
If not, you will have to go through dealings
You might end up apologizing more than twice
So always remember to say something nice, or have a good day
Express words of praise to the staff, children and parents at Sts. Peter and Paul
Never be unkind or hurtful to bring people to dismay
Nothing at all!
Say please, thank you and excuse me
Practice your good manners and happier you will be
Wherever you may be, you will certainly realize
That you will bring a smile to many, just wait and see
Imagine what a better world this will be
Just ideal!

~26~

Praise

Many times I praise other children
While I forget to praise my own
I need to start remembering
That charity starts at home
It's hard throughout the daily hurries
To take time to say, "I am proud of you."
Or just simply forget my worries
To see them through

Early One Morning

Early one morning
My three children were having breakfast
When I asked them,
"When I get older, if I get Alzheimer's disease what would you do with me?"
All three looked clueless,
While one shrugged his shoulders
They had no answer for me
I told them that when their dad started getting lost,
I was afraid he might end up homeless
For some poor homeless human beings might have started out the door one day
The poor forgetful people could not find their way back home again
As our loved ones get ill, forgetful and let strangers walk in the door
Also, innocently getting into cars with people they don't know
It is our responsibility and duty to keep our loved ones safe
and sound
For they need supervision and help
24/7

Do Right Unto Others

When you make other people happy
It comes back to you
That old fashioned saying
What goes around comes around
It's certainly true
Always do right unto others
All the good deeds you do
Will come back through
If you see a homeless person
Don't think of him or her as a bum
For they are misfortunate people
Who need help from gentle souls
Offer and give with respect
Just kindly say, "Sir or madam;
I have something I would like to share."
Here's a cool drink of juice or water
A loaf of bread and piece of fruit
Give and be gentle and always show respect
For you never know if it might be one of your loved ones
That may end up homeless

The Gift

Give thanks to your
Biological mother
For giving you the gift of life
Sometimes for different reasons
Your birth mother
Cannot raise you
That's why God blessed
Adoptive mothers
With the gift of an adoptive child
It's quite a responsibility
To raise a human being
Important daily decisions arise
Preparing healthy foods
Offering care, safety and affection
Selecting a good school
To get a good education
No matter how good or bad it gets
For better or for worse
In sickness and health
I'm certain that not even for
Millions of dollars
Would an adoptive parent
Trade you in

~30~

Judy K., Judy K.

During my lifetime, I've met Judy K. and Judy K.
They are both wonderful human beings
Special in every way
The first Judy K. I met, helps many children
She's very passionate about what she does
She is quite a Guardian Angel An Angel from above
All of the children that she has lent a hand to
Forever grateful they should be
For this Judy K. brought hope to their destiny
The second Judy K., is very special too
During working hours in the hospital
She helps very many people
During her time off
Instead of resting peacefully
She rescues many dogs
Many are Yorkshire Terriers
While some others are not

Mary Lou

Mary Lou is quite a bright lady
She is brilliant and quite assertive
She will defend people's rights
without even blinking an eye
She's helped many young and old
We want to communicate
We appreciate her so
So thank you Mary Lou,
For helping many members of my family
Without you it would have been much harder

The Wish

One Sunday afternoon
After our weekly visit to see my husband, my children's
dad
We were in the car when my youngest child, Alex said,
"Mommy if I could make a wish and ask God for
something,
I would pray that Papi could be okay and be home with us."
My daughter Anna quickly responded, "I know that's what
I always say."
My oldest son, Alberto agreed to the same
Their wish was not a toy, clothes or a trip to Disney World
What they wished for was for their father to get well
Alzheimer's is a progressive disease
A cure has not yet been found
Perhaps in the future the cure will be established
But for now all we can do, is keep him clean,
Loved, safe and sound

Don't Quit Now

Don't quit now
Just keep going
don't look back
Just keep on trying

Be hardheaded and have determination
with effort and sacrifice
the final outcome
will be worth the uphill struggle

Kind-Hearted

Good kind-hearted people
Come in every size and shape
Religion, creed or color
Won't stand in the way

God's Children

Black, white, yellow or red
we are all God's children in every way
He created us all
Special as can be
God loves us all, unconditionally

Teachers

Teachers were born to inspire,
Coach and prepare their students for the real world
Teachers that love what they do
Will reach up for the shining stars
The true stars are the learners
Who will be the future lawyers, doctors, teachers or whatever
their calling might be
Teachers shape the future and touch the lives of so many
A teacher can either make or break a child
If one is born to teach
One needs to handle with care the fragile minds of all of their
students
Treat the children with respect
Just like you expect them to treat you
We need to be firm, have discipline and have an open door
We need to treat our students
Just like we want other teachers to treat our own
Whether it's our sons, daughters or grandchildren

~37~

Bad Attitude

You might wake up one morning and meet someone with a
bad attitude
That person is angry and rude
Instead of getting to their level
Don't let them change your way
Just say, "I'm sorry you're having such a terrible day."
Pray for that person and hope that God gives them peace
Let's trust that with time
That person will have joy and will come to realize that
bitterness will only bring them loneliness
With courtesy and kindness
People will get closer to Heaven

Old Money, Or New Money?

When you see somebody with a lot of money
Do you wonder, is it new money or old money
If they've had it for two or more generations
That's old money
If not, it's new money

II. Nature

Pebbles

Pebbles, pebbles in the pond
Pebbles, pebbles everywhere
You don't have to wait until dawn
To find pebbles here and there
Let's throw the pebble far, far, far
And make it skip on the clean, clear water
What a lovely day to set our minds off worries
We giggled and laughed with great interactions
Finally we were very tired and sat to eat some berries

Blue Jay

Blue Jay, Blue Jay flying free
Watch out for the stray cat
Can't you see?
The hungry cat is a threat
You don't want to be his treat

Four Seasons

There are four glorious seasons in each blessed year
Winter, spring, summer, autumn, while some might call it fall
In the winter, go to the soup kitchens and help the less fortunate,
please volunteer
During spring would you like to smell the flowers or play
baseball?
Summer months are great to have fun in the sandy beaches.
Autumn is wonderful to watch nature's different colored leaves
fall
During autumn we go back to school where that awesome
teacher teaches

~45~

Mollusks

Mollusks have no skeletons
Some have shells for protection
Makes me think of gelatins
Do mollusks have a sense of direction?
Clams, octopuses, oysters, squids, snails
Can you name some others?
Mollusks eaten by the whales
Some survive with their sisters and brothers
Some mollusks live only in coral reefs
While some others live in the deep blue seas
Mollusks that survive must feel relief
In order to learn more and show expertise
Read an abundance of books about sea creatures
You can find more information by surfing the net
Ask your parents, friends and teachers
Encyclopedias and other resources, so you won't forget

III. Couplets

Poetry made up of two lines that rhyme

What a great day
When we went away

With close and good friends
You never need to pretend

I had a dream
That you were on, "The Dream Team"

Did you have a mental block?
When you went into shock?

Please go to the store to buy yellow squash
Just don't forget to take the cash

She started to complain
When she saw the chocolate stain

school rules

In all schools
They have classroom rules

IV. Just for the Fun of It

Pair Share

I can think of some names that come in pairs
If you'll give me a minute
I would like to share

Lucy and Ricky
Ethel and Fred
Laurel and Hardy
Mutt and Jeff
Fred and Wilma
Barbie and Ken
George and Martha

These are only a few of the very many
Can you think of any?

Adjectives for Body Parts and Organs

Enormous ears
Narrow nose
Fat fingers
Marvelous mouth
Tiny toes
Humble heart
Limp liver
Lovely lungs
Brilliant brain

Flavoring

Flavoring is great for the taste buds
Season your meat with salt
Wash your hands thoroughly until you see the soapsuds
Can you taste the ingredients in the malt?
Try a little cinnamon on your custard
Perhaps sugar in your tea
Hot dogs are great with mustard
Whether you are in land, air or sea

Lesson for a Happier Life

A	Adapt to Changes
B	Budget your income
C	Calm down
D	Delight others
E	Enhance your education
F	Focus while driving
G	Give thanks to God daily
H	Help others and yourself
I	Improve your talents
J	Jog if you can
K	Kindness to all
L	Love your family and friends
M	Make the best decisions

N	Nap if you are very grouchy
O	Open your heart to others
P	Praise your children
Q	Question what you know is wrong
R	Respect the young, old and homeless
S	Save for a rainy day
T	Try your best
U	Unite with all races
V	Value people's feelings
W	Welcome and appreciate others
X	X-ray broken bones
Y	Yearn for good health
Z	Zealous is a virtue, be passionate about your work

V. Haikus

Five Syllables, Seven Syllables, Five Syllables

This form of poetry originated in Japan.

My sweet small Yorkie
Loves Florida's bright sunshine
Her name is Lulu

Reflections in sight
such a wonderful delight
Leaves changing colors

Gushing waters flow
Feeling of serenity
Sunshine makes one glow

Two little mammals
Running as fast as they can
Spring is in the air

Dawn is getting near
Winter's cold is chilling us
Land, air, sea, plus fog

VI. Cinquains

Line one two syllables
Line two four syllables
Line three six syllables
Line four eight syllables
Line five two syllables

Education

What is?
Education
The power of knowledge
Wisdom, information, data
Culture

Family

Respect
Family bonds
Ancestors, relatives
Love and care for one another
Children

Friends

Loyal
Help each other
Through terrific and bad
True loving friends are forever
Trusting

Laughter

Laughter
Good for the soul
Let your worries be gone
Think of how you are blessed by God
Amen

Beaches

Beaches
Nice and sunny
Creative sandcastles
How relaxing and refreshing
Again

Blue

Blue is…
The sky's color
Waves breaking on the shore
Blue is my favorite color
What's yours?

Yellow

The sun
Bananas too
Crayons, markers, papers
Lemons are bitter and yellow
Also

Morning Breath

Bad Breath
Morning breath stinks
Go run and brush your teeth
Brush before and after you eat
Breakfast

Print Rich Environment

Billboards
Food cans' labels
Fast food restaurants' signs
Reading, reading always around
Print Rich

VII. Acrostics

Words or phrases added to; from a word spelled vertically

Stephanie

Super

Terrific

Exciting

Perfectionist

Happy

Amicable

Nice

Intelligent

Energetic

Ashley

Artistic

Sweet

Heartwarming

Loving

Entertaining

Youthful

William

Wonderful man

Intelligent person

Lively and fun to be with

Listens and guides

Interesting and warm

Advisor and full of wisdom

Meticulous about his job

Carlota

Caring

Admired

Religious

Loving

Organized

Terrific

Amicable

~90~

Mary

Marvelous as a piece of pie

Artistic and creative

Remembered as a loyal friend always

Youthful, funny and kind

Frances

Funny

Remarkable

Authentic

Noble

Capable

Enthusiastic

Stylish

Elsie

Exceptional

Loved

Special

Inspirational

Entertaining

VIII. Poems About Famous Inventors

Thomas Edison

Thomas Edison was such a great man
Before his inventions, there were only candles and gaslight
Surely it took many experiments and an outstanding plan
This great invention gave us better sight
Now we have a light bulb, thank goodness to him
We take it for granted, until the electricity goes out
Then the rooms look darker and quite dim
But please don't holler, scream and shout

Alexander Graham Bell

Thanks to Alexander Graham Bell
The members of many households today
Have lots to verbally ask and tell
By talking on the telephone everyday

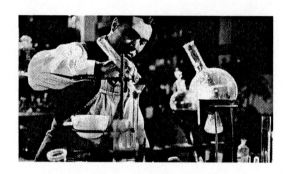

George Washington Carver

George Washington Carver
You were quite a scholar
Made over 100 products
From sweet potatoes and peanuts
Agricultural researcher
Chemical investigator
First science professor
That taught crop rotation
Honored by President Roosevelt

Henry Ford

When you think of a Ford
Whether it's a Thunderbird, Excursion or Mustang
Do you ever think of the man
That made it quite possible?
His name was Henry Ford
He had a vision
To have an assembly line
To assemble cars in mass production
He became very rich
By patenting his idea

~100~

IX. Alliterations

Repetition of the initial consonants

Silly Sally sings suspenseful songs

Annie apparently answers Albert and Alex about an arrow

Little Lulu likes licking lollipops

Carla can't carry countless cameras

Merry Mary marries marvelous Manny

Joyful Jason joins Jessica's jamming

Respectable Roger runs rapidly

Picky Patty puts peanut piles

Choosy child chose chopped chips

Terrific Terry takes tallies today

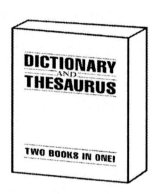

X.   *Synonyms*

Use a thesaurus

Find three or four words that mean the same for the first line

Then finish the poem with one more line

Mother, mommy, momma, mom
Regardless what you call her it means "love"

Homework, preparation, home learning
Complete and review thoroughly

XI. Limericks

Lines 1, 2 and 5 rhyme
While lines 3 and 4 rhyme

Wild Run

You should have seen such exciting fun
Right under the bright sun
There was a ferocious moose

Chasing a wild goose

We were all yelling, "Goose run, run, run!"

Sunflowers

The torrential showers
Beautified the colorful sunflowers
The flower fields were close to the bay
Sunshine was needed so we decided to pray
Prayers have many powers

Is It Easy or Hard?

Do you think it's hard or easy?
Or does it make you feel queasy?
To think of a great rhyme
Spend a little moment of your time
Are you feeling a bit uneasy?

Shooting Star

Have you ever been outside playing a guitar?
When all of a sudden you see a shooting star
The star was so bright
It was quite a sight
It seemed it was so close, but it was very far

XII. America, Land of the Free

Red, White and Blue

Thirteen stripes and fifty stars
Brave soldiers with severe scars
All wearing an identification tag
Standing proudly saluting the flag
Let us pray for peace and no wars

September Eleventh
911

September 11th will be a day many won't forget
Unthinkable news were on the television set
That dreadful day changed many lives
Lives of children, parents, husbands and wives
One should live with peace and not with threat

One Nation Under God

Thank God for freedom
Also for letting us have diversity
Stand proudly when singing the National Anthem
Get your education and go to the university
When standing up tall and proud
Recite *The Pledge of Allegiance*
Because we are allowed
Living in the U.S.A. is our preference

I Want to Live in America

Living in America is a delight
Each one of the fifty states
Is unique with its sights
When traveling compare hotels for different rates
Some states are full of sunshine
Others have fluffy white snow
As you're driving read the sign
to find what is the state's motto

~120~

The Flag

50 stars and 13 stripes
The colors are red, white and blue
The material used to sew them, are different types
The wind makes it flow freely and it's quite a view

Helpful Websites

http://www.alphaadvertising.com/covers/new1.html

http://www.barnesandnobleinc.com/for_authors/how_to_wor
k_with_bn/how_to_work_with_bn.html

http://www.bowker.com/

http://www.clipart.com/en/

https://www.lightningsource.com/index.htm

More Helpful Websites

www.cbcbooks.org/html/aboutauthors.html
www.childrenslit.com/f_mai.htm

www.dictionary.com
http://fairuse.stanford.edu/Copyright and Fair Use Overvi
ew/chapter8/8-a.html#1

http://www.loc.gov/poetry/180/p180-home.html

http://lcweb.loc.gov

www.msrogers.com/English2/poetry/30_days_of_poetry.htm
www.poeticbyway.com/glossary.html
www.poetry.com
http://poetry.i109.com/children'spoetry/
http://www.poets.org/

www.rhymer.com
www.rhymezone.com
http://write4kids.com

Index

Half Full,
Or
Half Empty?

A Collection of Poems

Written by

Ana Monnar

You will find a variety!
Narrative Poems
Couplets
Haikus
Alliterations
Limericks
Faith
Hope
Adoption
Determination
Responsibility
Kindness
Compassion
Nature
Famous
Inventors
Unity

Helpful websites are included, plus simple directions on how to write poems. This book will inspire some children to become young authors. Great for young adults!

Truly an educational literary piece of work!

~130~

About the Author

Ana Monnar was born on March 6, 1954 in Havana, Cuba. She is the oldest of four children. She moved to Miami, Florida at age seven. Since then, she became a U.S. citizen. Mrs. Monnar earned a Masters Degree in the area of Early Childhood and Elementary Education from Florida International University. Mrs. Monnar has been teaching for more than 25 years. She's taught second, third and fourth grades. She  also had the opportunity to work as a Reading Curriculum Specialist and Reading Leader. She has written successful grant proposals and earned the title, "Teacher of the Year" in the 1980's. Mrs. Monnar has inspired many learners to write Award winning pieces. Her students have won trophies and certificates for Regional and District Contests such as Young Authors, Books with Wings and Poetry Contests.

Mrs. Monnar married Octavio Monnar on August 20, 1982 and was later blessed with three children. Photography, reading, writing and going to the three children's activities are all fun and exciting diversions for the author. Throughout the years Mr. And Mrs. Monnar volunteered in The Children's Home Society. Caring for their Yellow Nape, Sunny and their loveable dogs Lulu and Pepe is a pleasure also. Lulu, the Yorkie featured on Readers Are Leaders U.S.A. was a rescue from Yorkshire Terriers of Mid America.

Readers Are Leaders U.S.A., Inc.
www.ReadersAreLeadersUSA.net

Printed in the United States
40133LVS00001B/105-106